BUSINESS RESEARCH: AN INFORMAL GUIDE

Rick C. Farr, Ph.D.
Paul R. Timm, Ph.D.

A FIFTY-MINUTE™ SERIES BOOK

CRISP PUBLICATIONS, INC.
Menlo Park, California

BUSINESS RESEARCH: AN INFORMAL GUIDE

Rick C. Farr, Ph.D.
Paul R. Timm, Ph.D.

CREDITS:
Editor: **Kay Kepler**
Typesetting: **ExecuStaff**
Cover Design: **Carol Harris**
Artwork: **Ralph Mapson**

Copyright © 1994 Crisp Publications, Inc.
Printed in the United States of America by Bawden Printing Company.

English language Crisp books are distributed worldwide. Our major international distributors include:

CANADA: Reid Publishing, Ltd., Box 69559—109 Thomas St., Oakville, Ontario Canada L6J 7R4. TEL: (416) 842-4428, FAX: (416) 842-9327

AUSTRALIA: Career Builders, P.O. Box 1051, Springwood, Brisbane, Queensland, Australia 4127. TEL: 841-1061, FAX: 841-1580

NEW ZEALAND: Career Builders, P.O. Box 571, Manurewa, Auckland, New Zealand. TEL: 266-5276, FAX: 266-4152

JAPAN: Phoenix Associates Co., Mizuho Bldg. 2-12-2, Kami Osaki, Shinagawa-Ku, Tokyo 141, Japan. TEL: 3-443-7231, FAX: 3-443-7640

Selected Crisp titles are also available in other languages. Contact International Rights Manager Suzanne Kelly at (415) 323-6100 for more information.

Library of Congress Catalog Card Number 93-73200
Farr, Rick C. and Paul R. Timm
Business Research: An Informal Guide
ISBN 1-56052-249-6

This book is printed on recyclable paper with soy ink.

ABOUT THIS BOOK

Business Research: An Informal Guide is not like most books. It stands out in an important way. It is not a book to read—it is a book to *use*. The "self-paced" format and many worksheets encourage readers to get involved and try new ideas immediately.

Finding information in a fast, accurate form is becoming crucial to the continuing success of today's organizations. In this "age of information," those who know how to obtain the answers to crucial business questions will increase their value to their company and enhance their professionalism. This book guides you in a step-by-step approach to basic research in business to gain and maintain that competitive edge.

Business Research: An Informal Guide (and other titles listed in the back of this book) can be used effectively a number of ways. Here are some possibilities:

- **Individual Study.** Because the book is self-instructional, all that is needed is a quiet place, committed time, and a pencil. By completing the activities and exercises, a reader receives both valuable feedback and action steps to improve your research skills and get the answers your organization needs.

- **Workshops and Seminars.** This book was developed from hundreds of interactive seminars and contains many exercises that work well with group participation. The book is also a refresher for future reference by workshop attendees.

- **Remote Location Training.** This book is an excellent self-study resource for managers, supervisors, and managerial candidates not able to attend "home office" training sessions.

Even after this book has been used for training and applied to real situations, it will remain a valuable source of ideas for reflection.

ABOUT THE AUTHORS

Rick C. Farr, Ph.D.

Dr. Farr is a consultant with extensive business experience in domestic and international business development, marketing and sales for emerging high tech companies. Dr. Farr obtained his Ph.D. degree from the Information Management Department at Brigham Young University after twenty years of practical management experience.

Paul R. Timm, Ph.D.

Dr. Timm is Chair of the Management Communication Department at the Marriott School of Management, Brigham Young University. He has authored 19 books and three video programs on communication, management, customer service and career management. He is an active consultant and trainer with corporate experience at Xerox Corporation and Bell South and scores of clients nationwide.

CONTENTS

PART 1: RESEARCH BASICS 1

The Importance of Research..3
The Nature and Scope of Business Research............................6
Ground Rules for the Business Researcher 13

PART 2: USING A RESEARCH MODEL 19

The Scientific Method 21
A Basic Model for Primary Research 22

PART 3: OBSERVATION TECHNIQUES 35

Observation in Research 37
Guidelines for Effective Observation 39
Specific Observation Techniques 41

PART 4: SURVEYS 47

Understanding Surveys...49
Preliminary Factors Necessary for Effective Surveys 54
How to Get a Random Sample...55
Questionnaire Design and Survey Administration...................58
Survey Applications in Business Research 68

PART 5: INTERVIEW TECHNIQUES 71

The Interview Process 73
Interview Formats..80

PART 6: EXPERIMENTS AND TESTS 89

Effective Tests and Experiments 91
The Game Is to Control the Variables..................................92
In Search of Validity and Reliability 94

APPENDIX: A SAMPLE RESEARCH INSTRUMENT 99

Organizational Communication Questionnaire Survey 101

PREFACE

Business more than any other occupation is a continual dealing with the future; it is continual calculation, an instinctive exercise in foresight.

—Henry R. Luce

Hotshot flyers of the World War I era bragged about ''flying by the seat-of-their-pants.'' But the barnstormer's life span was often short. Now we live in the high-tech age of supersonic travel and barnstorming just isn't good enough. It's reckless and potentially disastrous.

Likewise, business people today cannot rely on ''seat-of-the-pants'' guesses. Wrong guesses are too dangerous—too expensive. The need is to make better guesses and more informed predictions. The most effective way to make better guesses is by doing research.

The good news about using research techniques is that

> ✔ it is not difficult (although some people ''complexify'' it)
>
> ✔ it is fun
>
> ✔ it builds your professionalism

Learning the ideas presented in this book can have an enormous payoff. After all, how much more valuable is a good decision than a bad one?

No one can predict the future with absolute certainty. But with basic research techniques, the probability of success grows substantially.

So take off that leather helmet and flying scarf and slip into your 21st century flight suit. We're going to show you how to get the answers you need using this book as your guide.

Rick C. Farr

Paul R. Timm

P A R T

1

Research Basics

*66Business is never so healthy as when,
like a chicken, it must do a certain
amount of scratching for what it gets.99*

—Henry Ford

THE IMPORTANCE OF RESEARCH

Never have we needed a good crystal ball more than we do today. Yesterday's answers to business challenges no longer solve today's problems. Our society is undergoing fundamental changes as it shifts from the industrial age into the information age. Technology has and will continue to accelerate this change. The success of enterprise more than ever hinges on information—new ideas and strategies for providing goods and services. Information, carefully cultivated and used, is the lifeblood of every successful organization.

Because of this increasing emphasis on information, primary research skills are needed by managers, supervisors and anyone coping with today's business problems. Research isn't just for professors and graduate students. It is the key to good decisions and organizational effectiveness.

Research Skills Build Your Career Value

A recent survey done by the Administrative Management Society indicates that the ranks of middle managers have decreased by 25% over the last three years, largely because corporate leaders believe that layoffs in this area coupled with new technology will lead to greater productivity. What this means is that competition for the manager's job is increasing. People who want to ascend the corporate ladder will need to have modern skills. Just as the ability to obtain and use capital wisely was the mainspring of the industrial society, the ability to obtain and use information wisely will be the driving force behind the information age.

One of the manager's most important tools in obtaining information is primary research. People who are good researchers create a career advantage that will pay off handsomely.

THE PURPOSE OF RESEARCH

The purpose of research is to answer questions—to advance knowledge. A great deal of knowledge has been obtained through trial and error and chance experience. That method is a useful, but risky way of getting good answers.

In some cases, trial and error may be an acceptable option. Children learn basic skills by trying and failing until they get it right. There is no other way to learn how to walk or catch a ball.

A higher level of learning, however, uses logic, which leads to conclusions based on previous generalizations and experiences. Logical thinking puts different concepts together to form a new conclusion or concept. Research is simply a systematic way of doing this. It incorporates data-gathering methods to advance our understanding and make better decisions.

Here is a simple example you have probably experienced: If you decide to buy a new car, we doubt that you would just walk into the nearest dealer and grab the first car in sight. Instead, you would probably do some research. You might read stories in automobile magazines or consumer's guides to compare features. Perhaps you'll talk to friends who have recently bought new cars and ask about their experiences. You might even count the number and type of new cars you see on the streets, assuming that if a lot of people are buying a certain brand, it must be pretty good.

This is the kind of research you have been doing all along. The object of this book is to help you do more effective research.

Researching is not mysterious; it's not exceptionally complex. It can become a day-to-day activity that produces huge dividends in the form of good answers and good decisions.

A Quick Check of Your Research I.Q.

Answer the following true or false:

_____ **1.** Research takes many forms but is always systematic in its approach.

_____ **2.** Careful research is essential in solving any business problem.

_____ **3.** Research is a sophisticated science using precise methods only.

_____ **4.** Any problem can be solved with library research.

_____ **5.** Statistical analysis must be done to get any meaningful conclusions from research.

Author comments on Research I.Q.:

1. True
2. Not any problem, but many.
3. Not always. Some research is simply careful application of common sense.
4. False. The library is a good starting point for problems others may have experienced.
5. False. Much can be learned by simply "eyeballing" data.

THE NATURE AND SCOPE OF BUSINESS RESEARCH

Business research has four unique characteristics:

1. Business research is almost always applied research. This means that it is problem-oriented with the objective of obtaining information to help solve a specific business problem or make a decision.

2. Business research tends to have a time limit. It makes little sense to gather information about a decision that was made three weeks ago or to get information next week that we need today. Information is highly perishable. It gets old and useless very quickly. Like fish, if you don't consume it when fresh, it loses a lot of its flavor—and starts to smell bad!

3. Business research is done in an environment in which conditions change rapidly. The answers to research questions asked today may very well differ from the answers to the same questions obtained yesterday. In those areas where the manager needs to "stay in tune" with the changing landscape, the same research questions might need to be asked repeatedly. Successful organizations develop a culture where constant research is an integral part of their operation.

4. Business is a for-profit enterprise, so research must have some cost limits applied. Research can be expensive and time consuming (although many economical approaches can be used). If faced with a $10 problem, don't waste $1,000 on research. Likewise, a million-dollar decision must have a bigger budget for research than a $100 decision.

RESEARCH CAN BE CLASSIFIED AS PRIMARY OR SECONDARY

> For our purposes, the following definition will apply: *Research is the process of getting dependable answers to important questions using a systematic method of gathering, analyzing and interpreting evidence. Its end product is knowledge.*

When we search through publications (books, magazines, newspapers, pamphlets, government documents, atlases, encyclopedias, etc.) looking for answers to questions, we are doing what is called **secondary research.** The use of secondary research techniques allows managers to save their companies much time and money by avoiding unnecessary duplication. The attitude here should be, ''Why reinvent the wheel when it's so much easier to read about what others have already done?''

For many research questions, a literature search should be done first to find relevant data that will either answer the question outright or help refine it further. When you reviewed a copy of *Consumer Reports* before buying a car, you were using secondary research. A skilled librarian and some patient snooping around at a good library can help you in these efforts.

Let's assume, however, that the library research effort has not yet yielded a solid answer to the question. You've read the car magazine but still aren't ready to make a buying decision based on this information. You want to be certain that you are buying the best car for you.

Then you will find it necessary to do **primary research**—to collect primary data that must be obtained firsthand from nonpublished information sources. Such information comes from four sources:

- **OBSERVATIONS**
- **SURVEYS**
- **INTERVIEWS**
- **EXPERIMENTS**

In our car-buying example, you may well use all four. You will *observe* how well the car seems to be built, how it sounds, how it handles on the road. You may take an informal *survey* by *interviewing* some friends who have bought similar cars. You may even try an *experiment* where you'll try driving several cars over the same roads at the same speeds to see which handles better.

RESEARCH CAN ALSO BE CLASSIFIED AS BASIC OR APPLIED

Basic research seeks to further human knowledge about our world. This type of research does not necessarily solve a specific problem. Basic research sometimes is called ''pure'' or ''fundamental'' research. Scientists who study the laws of nature to understand these phenomena further are doing basic research. Business examples of such research questions may be ''How does population growth affect business cycles?'' or ''What are the relationships between weather and consumer behavior?'' These questions are the stuff of ''think tanks.''

Applied research, on the other hand, is problem-oriented. It seeks to solve specific problems by providing information that will facilitate an appropriate decision. Business examples: ''How will a 10% price increase affect our profits?'' or ''Where should we locate a new store, factory or distribution center?''

Applied research is what business people do to get the information needed for good decisions. With correct and accurate data, most business decisions become quite obvious.

TYPES OF RESEARCH

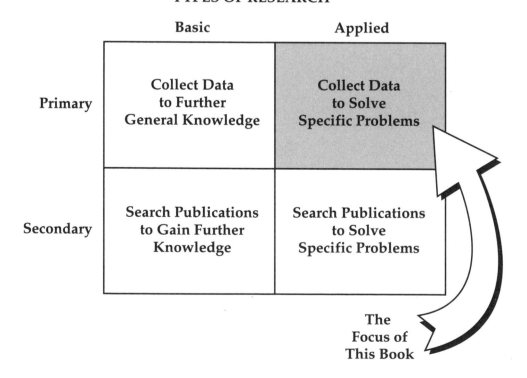

	Basic	Applied
Primary	Collect Data to Further General Knowledge	Collect Data to Solve Specific Problems
Secondary	Search Publications to Gain Further Knowledge	Search Publications to Solve Specific Problems

The Focus of This Book

Exercise: Your Turn

In the chart below, write an example from your organization of each type of research.

	Basic	**Applied**
Primary		
Secondary		

PROBLEMS FOR PRIMARY, APPLIED RESEARCH

The following are examples where primary, applied research can be useful in reaching a business decision. The sample research questions have been grouped within four business functions found in most companies.

I. Marketing

- What price should we charge for our product?

- What distribution channels should be used?

- How well does the product match up with the competitor's product?

- How effective is the company's advertising?

- How will this new product be received by the consumers?

- What percentage of market penetration does Product X have?

- What is Product X's image in the consumer's mind?

II. Finance

- What would be the market reaction to a new stock offering?

- How does that typical investor view the company?

- What is the market value of the fixed assets in the manufacturing division?

- Do most of the Fortune 500 companies use this procedure?

- What do the accounting supervisors think about the new computer installation?

III. Manufacturing

- Who is the most reliable vendor for this raw material?

- What is the most efficient plant layout and location for Product X?

- Does Product X meet the quality control standard?

- Would it be possible to substitute raw material Y for Z?

- What automated warehouse system should be purchased?

- What lighting system gives the highest increase in productivity?

- What is the exact nature of this production task?

IV. Personnel

- What skills are required for this job?

- What is the salary range for similar employees in this area?

- What type of training would be desirable for this job?

- How do employees feel about their job, the company and its management?

- How good is the communication among employees, supervisor and subordinates?

- Which employees are promotable?

Some of the above examples of research questions might be answered with secondary (library) research, but if the library doesn't offer a solid answer, be ready to find your own with primary research.

Exercise: Ask the Right Questions

List five business questions you'd like to have good answers for. Use the four business functions to jog your thinking. Be specific. Be certain these answers are worth the cost and effort that will be expended to get them.

My Top Five Business Questions:

1. _____

_____

2. _____

_____

3. _____

_____

4. _____

_____

5. _____

_____

GROUND RULES FOR THE BUSINESS RESEARCHER

The following six ground rules will help you avoid serious methodological mistakes at the onset of any primary research effort.

1. Always Know What You Are Researching

It is possible for researchers to get so wrapped up in acquiring new data that they forget to keep a specific research problem in the forefront of their minds. They go off onto tangents and diversions from the primary purpose of the study, delaying the research findings and the business decision.

The "80/20 rule" applies here. The research can obtain 80% of the needed information by focusing on the relevant and critical 20% of the research factors. In other words, to get 100% of the information, it will take five units of effort but to obtain 80% of the information, only one unit of effort is necessary. By confining your attention to only the most relevant questions and data, your research project can be accomplished faster with less cost than trying to do an all encompassing research effort.

2. Always Test a Research Model

A model is a conceptual representation of the project or plan. Just as a manufacturer wouldn't design a new product without first building several models, so should the researcher build a model first.

A model presents a framework from which to work. The structure is useful because it assures that the researcher, in the excitement to implement a project, does not overlook important steps, which, if not considered, might render the research worthless.

Using a pilot study is the best way to test a model. The pilot study, in which the researcher analyzes a small sample of data, quickly reveals any glitches in methodology. These glitches can then be fixed before the company spends a lot of time and effort on more extensive research. This is an example of using a model. Once the methodology is checked for soundness, the database can be reliably expanded. A big pile of untested data is useless.

GROUND RULES FOR THE BUSINESS RESEARCHER (continued)

3. Never Use Only One Information-Gathering Technique

No matter how scientific the data-gathering technique is, findings should be checked by at least one additional research method. For example, a survey research approach might well be validated by personal interviews. Systematic observations of people may be checked against their productivity reports. The two-technique approach is professionally known as the use of nonrepetitive, redundant measures. The adage is: If the research is worth doing, it is worth validating with a second approach. Or as the old carpenter used to say, "Measure it twice before cutting it once."

4. Use the KISS Principle

When it comes to studying a problem, **keep it short and simple** (KISS). Don't carry on an extensive research project simply for the sake of the research. Remember the objective is to get good data that is useful to a business decision. This data is to be obtained as quickly, efficiently and inexpensively as possible.

When a great deal of money is spent on an elaborate research project, people will have high expectations for the result. If the problem does not warrant that kind of effort, the natural consequence will be a big letdown.

Furthermore, the more complicated the project is, the more likely something will go wrong. Complex, multidimensional research can be difficult to administer and confusing to interpret. It is better to do a series of separate, little studies. Keep the apples and oranges separate.

5. If Necessary, Hire a Professional

If the research decision is critical to the company and requires complex statistical tools beyond your experience, get help from a statistician or a professional research designer. This is not as expensive or difficult as it might seem. Many large organizations have specialists on staff who are paid to be in-house consultants for such efforts. Don't be too ego-involved to get other people's ideas and expertise. Research is often a team effort.

For smaller companies or when an in-house specialist is not available, get help in the open market. Outside consultants are readily available. They are fast, efficient, and although seemingly expensive, they can save companies a great deal of time and effort.

An excellent source for technical help can be found on university campuses. Colleges and universities that offer graduate programs generally have students or faculty who will help with interesting research. A phone call or two will usually obtain a name of a qualified person who can resolve research design and statistical questions for a minimal cost.

Remember too that faculty members are often eager to research real world problems so they can publish their results in professional journals or share their experiences in the classroom. By so doing, they build professional credibility and promotion opportunities. This can be a win-win situation for them and for you.

DON'T FORGET THE FINAL RULE!

GROUND RULES FOR THE BUSINESS RESEARCHER (continued)

6. Make the Decision

Once the research has been completed, the manager should use the information to make a decision. It is important to do something with the research—don't just continue researching the problem to death. At some point you need to quit cutting bait and start fishing.

Decisions are never made with 100% certainty. The manager who procrastinates, using the need for more information as the excuse, does the company no service.

One could argue that there is always the need for more information, especially on high-cost decisions. But using that excuse because the manager is afraid to make a decision is irresponsible.

Primary research exists to make better decisions. When careful research points the way, make the decision without delay.

Exercise: Research Definitions

In your own words, define these terms:

Primary research:_____

_____

_____

Secondary research:_____

_____

_____

Applied research:_____

_____

_____

Basic research:_____

_____

_____

Research model:_____

_____

_____

KISS:_____

_____

_____

P A R T

2

Using a
Research Model

It is common sense to take a method and try it. If it fails, admit it frankly and try another. But above all, try something.

—Franklin D. Roosevelt

THE SCIENTIFIC METHOD

The scientific method describes a series of steps that researchers use to get answers to questions. The overall result of successful application of this method is almost always the best answer available.

The 10-Step Method

Usually, the steps are as follows:

1. Become aware of the problem, concern or question. (How did the issue come to light?)

2. Define the problem and purpose of research specifically. (What are the independent and dependent variables?)

3. Hypothesize about the causes and solutions to the problem.

4. Determine what information is needed to solve the problem.

5. Select methods for collecting information. (How?)

6. Collect data or evidence. (When, where?)

7. Compile data in systematic form. (How?)

8. Analyze findings to determine whether they support or contradict the hypotheses.

9. Prepare a research report to bring out full significance of findings and prescribe a course of action.

10. Follow up to be sure the solution works.

A more specific application of this scientific method is described in the basic model for primary business research.

A BASIC MODEL FOR PRIMARY RESEARCH

An application of the scientific method in the basic model of primary research (see the diagram below) is made up of five steps (boxes) and two decision points.

THE FIVE STEPS ARE:

1. State the problem

2. Check secondary sources

3. Do primary research

4. Make the decision

5. Check the outcomes

THE TWO DECISION POINTS ARE:

1. Do you have needed information?

2. Is the problem solved?

BASIC MODEL FOR PRIMARY RESEARCH

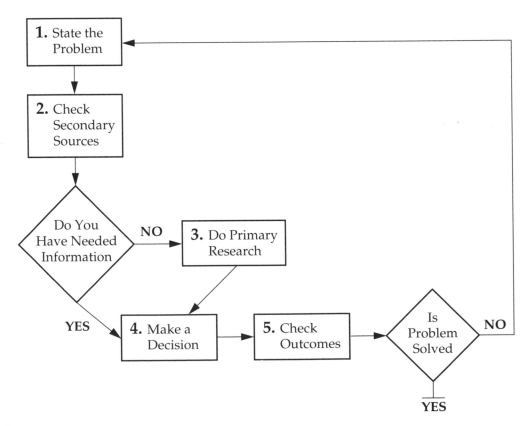

1. State the Problem

The first step in doing any research is to define the true nature of the research problem. What exactly do we want to know? Getting the right answers to wrong questions happens more often than you might think. Unless you are working directly on an explicitly identified problem, you really are not doing research, you are simply gathering information.

How do we know we have a problem? Problems come to light in a variety of ways, including:

- Customer complaints

- Conversations with company employees

- Observation of inappropriate behavior or conditions in the firm

- Deviation from the business plan

- Success of the firm's competitors

- Relevant reading of published material (This may reveal, for example, changes in market or environmental trends, new government regulations, anticipated changes in the economy, etc.)

- Company records and reports

Once the symptoms of a business problem appear, do some initial fact gathering that will help to determine the nature of the true problem. This fact gathering might include talking to others about the problem and conducting a preliminary literature search directly on the topic. This fact-gathering process is aimed at refining the researcher's educated guess to a more accurate problem statement.

During the initial investigation, the researcher must define the scope of the problem and try to determine the cause-and-effect relationships between the variables. (A ''variable'' is simply a factor that causes something to vary. For example, a sales variable might be a product's price, size, speed, color or anything else that can cause sales levels to vary.)

✔ *Action Step: Define My Research Problem*

Take a moment and define a specific research problem your organization is dealing with: (We will refer back to this problem in exercises later in the book.)

_____

_____

_____

_____

_____

_____

_____

_____

_____

_____

_____

_____

_____

_____

_____

_____

_____

_____

_____

_____

_____

Phrasing a Researchable Problem

To state a problem that can be researched, it is necessary to write it into a form that includes the following factors:

- A relationship between two variables, or possibly among several variables, is questioned

- Each variable is operationally defined, either within the problem statement or in supplemental statements to it

- A population for the research is implied or identified

Here is an illustration of these factors as applied to a poorly worded research question. The question, ''I wonder why our company's sales seem to be leveling off?'' is essentially not researchable for a number of reasons. It does not clarify:

▶ What relationships are described?

▶ How do we know sales are ''leveling off''?

▶ ''Leveling off'' compared to what?

This research question suffers because the terms are not specifically defined. When we say ''sales,'' do sales refer to Product X or Products Y and Z? (Maybe X and Y are selling in record numbers, but Z is pulling down the overall results.) Does ''leveling off'' mean that the growth of sales is slower than in the past or that there is no growth at all?

Finally, what population is implied? Do we mean all sales to all customers or particular types of sales to a certain population of customers?

Operational Definitions

An operational definition is a definition that is determined by the operations needed to measure it. If that sounds like doubletalk, slow down and read it again. What operations are needed to define a thing? What, specifically do we need to do to classify a thing?

If we assume that a term we use is universally known or has only one meaning, we are heading for trouble. In our early example about buying a car, what do I mean by a car? You probably know what you mean, but for research into cars, we'd need to define exactly what a car is. Does your definition include pickup trucks and sports utility vehicles like a Ford Explorer or Chevy Blazer? How about mini-vans—are they cars too? If you want to compare foreign to domestic cars, you open a can of worms that even professional researchers have trouble sorting out. Is a Toyota built in Kentucky or a Honda built in Ohio a domestic car? Is a Chrysler built in Canada a foreign car?

Exercise: Creating Operational Definitions

Operational definitions reduce ambiguity. Fill in the table below to operationalize these definitions.

Term	Operational Definition
CUSTOMER	One who visits the store and purchases items [Note the operations needed to qualify as a customer: "visit store" and "purchase"; a browser wouldn't count.]
SUPERVISOR	An employee who has one or more employees reporting directly to him or her.
PREFERRED CUSTOMER	
SUCCESSFUL PRODUCT	
LOW MAINTENANCE	
SATISFIED WORKER	
ACCURATE WORK	
QUALITY CUSTOMER SERVICE	

A BASIC MODEL FOR PRIMARY RESEARCH (continued)

Looking for Relationships (in all the right places)

After knowing your operational definitions, it is important for a research problem to have a relationship between two or more variables. The sample statement, "I wonder why our company sales have been leveling off?" does not compare the minimum of two variables.

A better problem statement would be, "Has the cutback in print advertising for Product X [one variable] resulted in a decline in sales growth [another variable] over the last six months [still another variable]?" In the new statement, the independent variable—cutback in print advertising—is hypothesized as having made a change in the dependent variable—sales over the past six months.

Let's clarify "independent" and "dependent." An independent variable is something that we can control. In this example, we can control the amount of print advertising. The "dependent" variable depends on, or, we might guess, is caused by changes in the independent variable.

The problem statement could be further improved by spelling out the relationship between the two variables and stating how the variables' advertising and sales were to be measured.

An improved research question might become, "Has the 50% reduction in Product X's January to December 19XX print advertising resulted in the low 1% sales growth of Product X for the six months of July through December 19XX?"

The population for this research question would be the buyers and potential buyers of product X during the past six months.

This statement is now correct and is researchable because all variables are related, measured and specific.

2. Check Secondary Sources

Once the research problem has been clearly stated, we can do the second step of the model—check secondary (library) sources. Remember that primary research can be time-consuming and expensive, so finding answers to previously asked questions is always preferable—as long as it applies directly to your business question. In some cases, you will find such information through a library search. Business problems that are not unique may have been answered, and the results published, by someone else. If the published case is similar to yours, you may have the answer you need.

✔ *Action Step: Ask Secondary Research Questions*

Apply these questions to the research questions you identified on page 24.

1. Who might have researched this question before?_____

_____

_____

2. How might you make direct contact with the individuals who research the question?_____

_____

_____

3. Where might a solution to this problem be published? (What possible publications?)_____

_____

_____

4. What government agency would also need to have the answer to this question?_____

_____

_____

5. What vendors might be able to help with information on this topic?_____

_____

_____

6. What reference library could I call?_____

_____

_____

A BASIC MODEL FOR PRIMARY RESEARCH (continued)

We saw an interesting example of using secondary research by a marketing manager for a high technology company. He was asked to determine how much additional acreage in the continental United States could become tillable—if a zero-cost energy source were available. Apparently, his company had been doing theoretical work in the area of nuclear fusion and needed this type of information. To answer this unique question could take months and cost thousands of dollars, but this researcher had the answer within an hour. After making five calls, he reached an individual in the U.S. Department of Agriculture in Washington, D.C., whose job it was to calculate such information.

Librarians are available to help in such searches. That's what they are there for. Use their expertise.

Always use secondary research methods first. If the library does not yield a solution to the research problem, the effort will have at least helped to clarify and perhaps redefine the research problem. Often a review of similar problems in published sources gives new ideas on your topic.

3. Do Primary Research

As you move into primary research, think through the following steps to ensure a systematic approach.

▶ **Establish Limits on Time and Money.**
How much time should reasonably be spent on researching this question? If the need is urgent, a limited "quick and dirty" study may be all that one can do. If the problem has been identified early and the time is available to make a more thorough analysis, all the better. Likewise, if the costs of ignoring the problem are huge (say, the company could go under if we don't do something), spending any amount of money to get good answers would be reasonable.

Of course, few questions are quite that big or urgent. So management must decide how much to spend for the answers needed.

When figuring expenditures, remember to figure in costs of the researchers' time, printing and copying, computer time for data analysis and hiring of outside experts as needed.

If Primary Research is Required

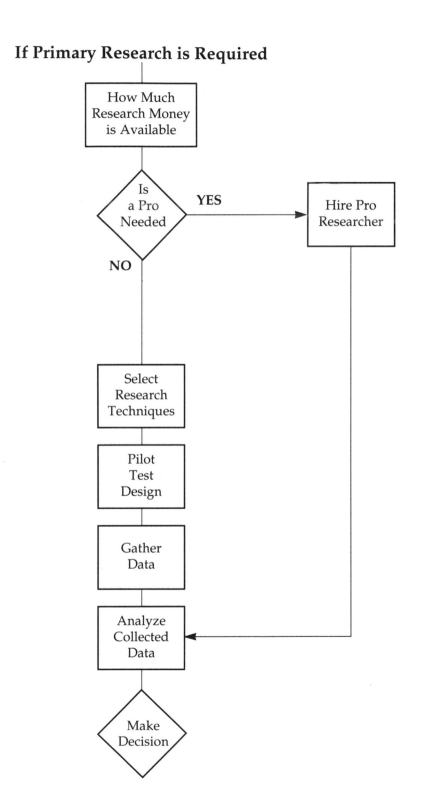

A BASIC MODEL FOR PRIMARY RESEARCH (continued)

▶ **Determine if a Professional Researcher Is Needed.**

▶ **Determine Research Techniques Needed.**
Most problems faced by businesses can be researched using the four techniques described in this book: observation, survey, interview or experiment. Some combination or variations on these may be useful, but these techniques can get the answers needed in most of cases.

▶ **Pilot Test Data Gathering Techniques.**
Try out the chosen method on a sample before using unproven approaches on a larger population.

▶ **Gather Data.**

▶ **Analyze the Data.**
Raw data is not the end product of research, it is an intermediate step toward a decision. To refine raw data into information, we must accumulate a sufficient amount, summarize and digest it.

---

4. Make a Decision

The last activity in the basic model of primary research is making a decision based on the research coupled with the manager's own good judgment.

---

5. Check the Outcomes

The ultimate proof in the pudding is whether or not the decision worked. After a reasonable amount of time, retest to see if the decision made has solved the original problem. If not, it's back to square one.

✔ *Action Step: Outline Problem-Solving Steps*

Create a research plan. Refer back to the problem you described on page 24 and outline the steps you'll take to complete systematic research into the problem. Refer back to the model. Name people and outside sources you may wish to use.

1. _____

   _____

2. _____

   _____

3. _____

   _____

4. _____

   _____

5. _____

   _____

6. _____

   _____

7. _____

   _____

8. _____

   _____

9. _____

   _____

10. _____

    _____

PART

3

Observation Techniques

"You can observe a great deal just by watching."

—Yogi Berra

OBSERVATION IN RESEARCH

Perhaps you never thought of ''just watching'' as a research technique. It can be, although only if done with a planned purpose. All people observe their environment to some degree, which is one reason observation is so frequently used to gather data. Although it is so commonly employed, observation is also the most difficult data-gathering technique to use correctly, because research observation involves much more than casual viewing and a haphazard absorbing of information.

For observation to qualify as a valid research method, it must be used systematically and analytically. Topics, objects or systems targeted for observation must be clearly and narrowly decided before work begins. If the variables are not clearly defined, the observer might note one set of items during one observation and another set during another observation. Define your criteria to avoid this trap.

It's what you learn after you know it all that counts.
—John Wooden

OBSERVATION IN RESEARCH (continued)

Advantages of Observation Techniques

1. Systematic observation provides more accurate information than can be obtained haphazardly or through casual observation. The observer will obtain data firsthand rather than filtered through the thoughts and opinions of others. Done correctly, the process reduces most bias and distortions.

2. Using observation techniques in connection with mechanical devices (such as rulers, timeclocks or gauges) can produce the most accurate possible data. Any system that produces hard data and consistent measurement will go a long way in eliminating bias and interpretation errors from the study.

3. Observation data is real-world data, not data from a laboratory study designed to duplicate real life. Observations mirror situations as they really exist.

4. Observation is that the results of the study can be readily verified. Managers can check the results through similar observation techniques, and repeated observations can validate the original findings.

Disadvantages of the Observation Technique

1. If observers have not been carefully trained, the data may reflect observer biases.

2. Observers may spend a lot of time and effort noting the routine, insignificant event. The unusual, and potentially useful, data is often hidden under a mountain of trivial observations.

3. Observation techniques are of no value when researchers need to know about people's feelings and attitudes. Observations require behavior or tangible evidence of actions. Much of what managers need to know involves how people feel about situations, services, products and the like.

You can't generally observe a thought or feeling. We can infer attitudes from behaviors, but the link between the two is often tenuous. To get at peoples' feelings and attitudes, look instead to surveys. (See Part 4.)

GUIDELINES FOR EFFECTIVE OBSERVATION

Be sure the observer is fully prepared. The person making the observations must clearly understand the operational definitions used in the study. In addition:

1. Prepare in advance the forms used to record the data. Pretest these with a pilot study to be sure the observers know exactly how to record observations. A pilot study will help you iron out any glitches in the data-gathering techniques or forms.

2. Use objective observers, not people who may have a bias. If, for example, you are observing work behaviors in a particular department, use observers who work elsewhere or, better yet, do not know the people being observed. Be sure, however, that these observers do know how to recognize desirable behaviors. The operational definitions become important.

3. Prepare in advance a schedule of all observations. Indicate who will observe, where to observe and when to observe.

4. Train all observers carefully. Be sure they know what to look for and what behaviors are not vital. During the training process, observers should use the same recording forms and be thoroughly instructed on how to complete them.

5. If employees are observed, they should be informed of the process and reasons for the observations. No one likes to have a person with a clipboard hovering around—especially when the employee doesn't know why. Besides, people's behaviors change when they know they are observed.

GUIDELINES FOR EFFECTIVE OBSERVATION (continued)

▶ **Be sure the observations are systematic and methodical.**
The entire observation process must be planned to get good data. Many things can bias the data and render it worthless. By systematizing in advance precisely what, when and where observations will be made, you reduce the chance of distorting the information needed to make a good decision.

To ensure systematic observation, use carefully designed forms and gather enough observations at different times to achieve a representative cross-section of the population observed. For example, if you need to observe salespeople at work, you'll want to see them during different times of the day, under different customer conditions, during busy and slow times, etc.

Make your observations methodical by always recording data the same way. Although we often think of simply tallying observations on a clipboard, some situations may call for measuring devices such as counters, stop watches, computers, cameras, video recorders and other mechanical devices. Be certain that your observers are well trained in the use of these methods.

▶ **Attempt to make the observation process unobtrusive.**
The observer must minimize his or her presence in the observation process. If the observer is blatant in observing and recording data, the people being observed may act differently than normal, thus masking what really goes on in the company. Studies have shown that the very presence of the observer can lead to improved performance in the short run. This is called the "Hawthorne effect," named after a factor where it was first noted.

Exercise: Observation Techniques

Describe a problem where observation techniques make sense. Summarize what you'll do to avoid observation research errors.

The problem: _____

I'll avoid observation errors by:

1._____

2. _____

3. _____

SPECIFIC OBSERVATION TECHNIQUES

Time and Motion Studies

This approach has long been used to analyze actions needed to complete a task. Here is an example.

Suppose that you have a few workers who produce substantially more than the typical person in that job. You may want to use this observation technique to evaluate what the high producers do and compare their movements with those of the less productive workers. When you think you have figured out why the good workers are so good, you can teach other workers the same skills.

In addition to using time and motion studies to increase productivity, they can also be used to determine manufacturing costs of a new product or to develop work schedules.

Behavioral Frequency Counts

This observational approach focuses on how often particular behaviors occur during normal day-to-day actions. For example: One study compared the behaviors of top salespeople to the behaviors of the rest of the salesforce. Using behavioral frequency counts, the observers found that the best salespeople listened longer, asked more probing questions and requested the order more often than the average salesperson.

SPECIFIC OBSERVATION TECHNIQUES (continued)

Reports and Other Written Documents

Another way managers can use observation techniques is to review written documents. A great deal of data can emerge from a systematic study of records, reports, memos and letters.

Most major telephone companies use this technique in conjunction with recording customer conversations. Any commitments or promises made by the service representative are noted, and the service observer then searches the company's records to see if these commitments were met.

Companies routinely maintain production records that provide information on downtime, budget variances, absenteeism, tardiness, output, terminations, work stoppages, overtime and many other factors. Systematic checking of such data using observational techniques can answer many business questions.

Since such data has already been collected, the researcher's job is simply to reformat and summarize the data. To use existing company records, the following approach is recommended:

1. Identify and locate appropriate records.

2. Determine how large a sample will be needed to reflect the true problem.

3. Develop a collection plan that defines which data is to be collected, who will collect it and where it will be collected.

4. Gather the sample and transcribe usable data from current records onto a summary form.

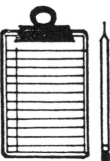

Tallying Observation Behaviors

Use simple check sheets to record observations. A check sheet is an easy-to-understand form used to answer the question, "How often are certain events happening?"

Once you've determined what is to be observed and recorded, you'll need to decide how often and for how long observations will take place. Design the check sheet to be clear and easy to understand. A sample salesperson behaviors check sheet is shown below.

Observed Behaviors

	Greets Customer Promptly	Makes Small Talk	Asks Key Questions	Gives Info/ Assistance	Explains/ Clarifies Features	Asks for Order	Writes the Order
Salesperson 1							
Salesperson 2							
Salesperson 3							

Exercise: Design Your Checksheet

Using the blank form, design a checksheet that can be used to tally behaviors you would like to see in salespeople. Identify the behaviors in the boxes across the top of the form. Then tally behaviors you see. If you are not in a sales organization, test this sheet by observing sales behaviors directed at you as a customer.

Salesperson 1							
Salesperson 2							
Salesperson 3							

Case Study: What's Going On Here?

Imagine yourself walking into the machine shop of a small but not very profitable manufacturing company. It's 9:30 a.m. on a Tuesday, but the place is quiet. Only three people are there. One man is sitting on a bench next to his machine, leaning against the wall. He has a blank look on his face. Another employee is fixing a child's bicycle. The third person is talking to someone on the phone whom he addresses as "Honey." What do your immediate impressions tell you about this scene?

Write out two or three conclusions you could draw from these observations. What is going on?

1. _____

_____

_____

_____

_____

2. _____

_____

_____

_____

_____

3. _____

_____

_____

_____

_____

Case Study Review

We wouldn't be surprised if you said something like, "A bunch of goof-offs work here." "These workers are taking advantage of their job; not producing what they are paid for." "I bet their supervisor is away." "I'd probably fire them if they worked for me."

Maybe you'd be right, but here is what was really happening in that shop: The first employee had worked all night to get out a rush order, an order that will result in a major profit increase for the company. He hadn't slept in more than 24 hours and was taking a 15-minute break. The man on the phone had also been working through the night. This was the first chance he'd had to call his wife to see how their sick four-year-old daughter was responding to some new medication. The third worker was taking time on his normal day off to work on the company-sponsored "Toys for Kids" Christmas project.

Did you perhaps jump to the wrong conclusions? Therein lies the danger of haphazard, unstructured observations. They can be wrong—dead wrong, despite convincing evidence to the contrary.*

Have you carefully considered all the pieces before reaching a conclusion?

---

*This description originally appears in *Supervision*, 2nd Edition, by Paul R. Timm. St. Paul, MN: West Publishing. 1993. pp. 46–47.

P A R T

4

Surveys

❝How dangerous it is to reason from insufficient data.❞

—Sherlock Holmes

UNDERSTANDING SURVEYS

Surveys may be the most widely used and abused information-gathering technique. They are widely used because people think they are easy to do. But as with most things, there are surveys and, then again, there are accurate surveys.

If a survey instrument is well written, pretested and administered properly, the study can yield a great deal of rich information about such things as organizational needs, problems, employee perceptions and consumer attitudes.

Questionnaires can be very cost effective, but the initial development of a useful instrument may be more expensive than anticipated if done carefully. In other words, questionnaires may not be as easy or inexpensive as you think.

Because a survey questionnaire can be written rather easily, this technique is often used instead of a more in-depth and difficult research approach. This "quick and dirty" image causes some researchers to discount the answers they may get from a survey. However, the survey approach has tremendous advantages for the business manager if it is designed and implemented properly.

Generally, the use of a questionnaire should be limited to research projects where information from other methods is not available. It could also be used to verify results generated from other methods.

Surveys are often mailed or otherwise distributed directly to the people who are asked to respond. They work best when the respondent knows that answers will be kept confidential.

Mailed surveys are useful when collecting data from people who may be geographically dispersed, such as customers across the country. This kind of sample often rules out the use of interviews (except by telephone), observations and experiments.

SURVEY ADVANTAGES

UNDERSTANDING SURVEYS (continued)

Advantages to the Survey Technique

► **They are inexpensive.**

Surveys are usually less expensive than observations, interviews and experimentation because they are not as labor-intensive. Once designed, a questionnaire can gather a large quantity of data without requiring a lot of employee time and, therefore, expense.

► **They are easy to administer.**

Since the questionnaire is an instrument that requires a written response, the administrator does not have to be skilled in interviewing or observing techniques. Generally, a simple group explanation of the questionnaire purpose or an explanatory letter will suffice.

► **Responses may be kept confidential.**

Data may be more accurate, since most respondents will be frank and honest when their answers are anonymous. (Technically, questionnaire responses are anonymous only if there are no identifying marks on the survey that could be associated with the respondent. If the surveys are numbered or request the respondent's name or other identification, the person should be told that answers will be ''confidential''; that is, what they say will not be associated with their name, except possibly by the researcher. The most sensitive issues are better handled via anonymous surveys.)

► **Most information received from questionnaires is quantitative and easy to process.**

Open-ended questions can be used to get unstructured responses, but we prefer the interview method for gathering such data, since people often have trouble clearly expressing themselves in writing.

► **Because surveys are used regularly, people are familiar with the tool, thus making it easy to take.**

► **Respondents may take time in thinking about the appropriate response.**

They won't face time pressures sometimes present in interviews.

► **Management tends to be receptive to the questionnaire approach.**

Data so gathered is usually seen as credible, as long as the survey is designed and administered properly.

UNDERSTANDING SURVEYS (continued)

Disadvantages of the Survey Technique

▶ **Survey questionnaires are impersonal and structured.**

Questionnaire instruments are one-way communications that generally do not allow respondents to clarify answers. This forced-choice format makes data processing easy, but if the researcher is asking the wrong questions or not allowing for a full range of responses, the data will be contaminated.

Suppose, for example, that a researcher *assumes* that respondents feel generally positive about the company's benefit program. He asks people to rate the benefits by circling one of the following responses: exceptional, excellent, very good, good, adequate.

Two problems could arise. First, the choices available may not cover what the respondent wants to say (they are too structured). Second, the respondent may be very happy with some aspect of the benefit package (for example, medical coverage), but very unhappy with another part (dental coverage). Survey questionnaires normally do not give people the opportunity to provide unstructured feedback or to elaborate on why they chose a particular rating.

▶ **The questionnaire may be subject to overinterpretation.**

Some people try to psychoanalyze every question. They read meaning into the question that was not intended and sometimes try to guess at how the researcher would like them to answer. For some people, the survey creates a "test" environment. They feel that they are being evaluated.

▶ **The process can be time consuming, especially if the questionnaire is sent through the mail.**

Allow ample time for people to respond. Put a due date on the survey but don't be surprised if responses dribble in well beyond that date.

▶ **Low response rates are common with mail surveys.**

Although many people can be reached at a relatively low cost with mail surveys, a major disadvantage is a low response rate. Many recipients will simply ignore a mail survey.

▶ **Responses can be distorted.**

Sometimes the only people who respond are those with extremely negative or extremely positive feelings. The more moderate respondent is unmotivated.

Exercise: Overcoming the Disadvantages

The disadvantages of surveys can be reduced or eliminated with a bit of creativity. Below, jot down your ideas for doing so. Then look at the authors' comments for other thoughts.

1. The *impersonal and structured* problem could be reduced by:

_____

_____

2. The *overinterpretation* problem could be reduced by:

_____

_____

3. The *time consuming* problem could be reduced by:

_____

_____

4. The *low response rate* problem could be reduced by:

_____

_____

5. The *distortion* problem could be reduced by:

_____

_____

Author's Suggestions:

If your ideas didn't include these, give them some thought too. Impersonalization problems can be reduced by giving respondents clear oral instructions (if administering the survey personally) or using a conversational, friendly tone in written instructions. Overinterpretation can be reduced by instructing people to give their first impressions and not to attempt to analyze the questions. A slow response rate can be reduced by administering the survey to larger groups of people (if possible) and by budgeting enough time to allow for mail delays if you use mail surveys. Response rates can be improved by rewarding the respondent with a token of appreciation. Some surveyors attach a dollar bill to a mail survey, others offer to make a donation to a charity if the person will complete the survey. Finally, the distortion problem can be overcome by recontacting nonrespondents by phone or follow-up mail, to assure them their input is needed.

PRELIMINARY FACTORS NECESSARY FOR EFFECTIVE SURVEYS

Some factors must exist before a good survey questionnaire can be developed.

1. The researcher must determine specifically what information is needed to meet the purpose of the research project.

2. The researcher must determine that the survey approach will be the best method for collecting the needed information. Be sure that the survey method represents the best choice among the other data-gathering approaches.

3. Before a survey project is implemented, the researcher must have a good understanding of the population from which the sample for the survey will be drawn. If the entire population (for example, all your customers, all vendors) or a random representative sample cannot be obtained, the data generated from this survey will be suspect.

If your whole population is small—say 300 or fewer—it is crucial to get a fairly high response rate. Experts differ on the level of response necessary for reliability, but here is a suggested range for smaller populations:

- 60% or Better   Very Good

- 35%–59%   Good

- 25%–34%   Questionable

- Below 25%   Unreliable

Larger populations can be randomly surveyed. Good results can come from as few as 383 out of a population of up to 1 million! (See pages 65 and 66 for more on sample size.)

HOW TO GET A RANDOM SAMPLE

Randomness means that any member of the population has an equal chance of being selected for the survey. If your population is defined as people who bought Ford trucks during May of this year, all such buyers have an equal chance of getting your survey. To ensure randomness, use one of these methods:

Method #1   Assign a number to each member of your population. If you have 173 truck buyers, number them from 1 to 173. Put slips of paper into a hat numbered 1 through 173. As your sample is drawn (suppose you decide to mail surveys to 50 people) check off each name and make your mailing list.

Method #2   A better approach is to use a table of random numbers. This table is computer-generated to ensure randomness. To use this, determine that you will select every third number until you have a full sample. Close your eyes and point to the starting number in the table. Then go down three numbers at a time, selecting your sample. (Drop off digits as necessary. We'd use only three digits in our example because our population is 173 truck buyers.)

Once you select a sample, stick with it. Substituting hurts randomness and a nonrandom sample is less reliable than a random one.

HOW TO GET A RANDOM SAMPLE
(continued)

If carefully selected, a random sample has the best probability of speaking for the whole population of any sample. If you cannot be assured of randomness, it would be best to survey the whole population. That wouldn't be hard in our truck buyers example, but would, of course, be extremely expensive for a population such as all truck buyers nationwide.

Table of Random Numbers

36137	42353	54264	01762	61844	70478
06511	50555	87031	32226	42361	48347
37411	30100	36383	78007	66760	02174
30546	17725	62862	63685	76105	46505
06835	07275	12563	43065	88713	15740
88566	78315	62044	77273	16241	42366
65011	14340	00533	77803	55314	37830
82448	66127	10637	62102	34488	50540
87276	62510	57557	61311	73472	71307
42334	88658	86130	87774	87348	76370
60030	05273	17186	18085	53333	81380
32731	43430	18565	15152	07581	23345
60056	28174	73801	16715	03554	50361
14280	52838	70656	28544	11240	47287
87108	68520	58574	13431	07222	70347
37816	84081	70116	86746	40372	78482
33137	37472	52371	28624	07705	50431
30067	87815	42464	43565	70036	74212
88452	32535	25765	28328	67145	05581
05657	73664	15566	25247	18880	35164
50001	86550	23353	38668	37308	05322
16084	13312	67676	13183	04768	76075
15010	07607	66471	20070	28838	66076
25056	85756	58287	27221	37367	31558
10851	53574	23084	00730	65464	28740

Exercise: Finding a Random Sample

1. Using the table of random numbers, identify a random sample size of ten out of a possible 99. Assume that your starting number is 36137 (the first number in the upper left corner of the table) and moving down the column using the first two digits of each number. Use every third number.

_____

_____

2. What would you do if you got duplicate numbers?

_____

_____

Once a sample has been identified, determine the survey technique to be used. This chapter will discuss the most common techniques that lend themselves to business use. Although more complex approaches are available, these techniques can be readily and profitably used by business people.

EENIE
MEENIE
MYNIE
MOE

Answers:

1. The correct answers are respondents number: 36, 30, 65, 42, 60, 37, 88, 16, 10.

2. Skip to the next selection—three numbers down.

QUESTIONNAIRE DESIGN AND SURVEY ADMINISTRATION

The following steps should be followed in designing a questionnaire:

1. **Determine the information wanted and types of questions needed.**

2. **Draft and develop the questions.**

3. **Test the questions.**

4. **Develop the complete questionnaire.**

5. **Determine the sample size you need.**

STEP 1: **Determine the Information Wanted and Types of Questions Required**

Rule #1: Know What You Are Researching. Be sure you have a clear picture of what you want to get from the survey. Avoid the temptation to toss in a few extra questions that may be interesting but are not germane to your study. Keep it focused. The longer the survey, the lower your response rate is likely to be.

Next, determine what questions would provide the most accurate data. Be sure to consider how the data will be tabulated and analyzed. Five types of questions are most frequently used in survey questionnaires. A questionnaire might have any or all of these types of questions.

► **Close-ended questions.** This question uses an either/or or yes/no response.

Examples:

- I have good communications with my supervisor.

  ☐ Yes   ☐ No

- The color scheme in our new store is generally

  ☐ attractive   ☐ not attractive

► **Open-ended questions.** This type of question allows the respondent to give an unlimited answer. The question should be followed by sufficient space for the response.

Examples:

- What problems are you having communicating with your supervisor? (Follow by space to respond.)

- Please describe how you most often use your new widget. (Follow by space to respond.)

Open-ended responses are difficult to quantify. They can be used in surveys to get ideas, examples and general feelings, but typically an interview is a better medium for this, since it allows the researcher to probe and clarify responses.

► **Checklist.** This type of question presents a list of items where participants are asked to check those that apply to their particular situation.

Examples:

- Please check the following types of communications that you have with your supervisor:
  - ☐ Informal meetings
  - ☐ Formal meetings
  - ☐ Written report
  - ☐ Letters
  - ☐ After-hours discussions
  - ☐ Telephone
  - ☐ Social gathering
  - ☐ Committee meetings

- Please check bank services that you have used (check as many as apply):
  - ☐ MasterCard
  - ☐ Checking
  - ☐ Certificates of deposit
  - ☐ Financial planning
  - ☐ Personal loans
  - ☐ Savings account
  - ☐ Home mortgages
  - ☐ Safe deposit box

QUESTIONNAIRE DESIGN AND SURVEY ADMINISTRATION (continued)

► **Multiple-choice question.** This type of question offers several choices and the respondent is asked to select the most correct one.

Example:

About how often do you purchase items from the company vending machines?

    (a) once a day or less

    (b) two–three times a day

    (c) three–five times a day

    (d) six or more times a day

To be effective, the choices presented must cover all possible options. Respondents get irritated when their selection isn't one of the options. (You can add a "none of the above" easily enough, although it won't tell you much.)

► **Ranking scales.** This type of a question requires the participant to rank order a list of items.

Example:

Of the following list of five types of communications that you might have with your supervisor, please place a 1 by the most important item to you, a 2 by the item that is second-most important, and so on. All five items should be ranked.

    ____ Formal meetings

    ____ Informal conversations

    ____ Written reports

    ____ Letters or memos

    ____ Telephone discussions

▶ **Likert scales.** This method is generally used to measure attitude toward a concept or idea. It allows the respondent to agree, disagree or indicate the degree of agreement (usually on a five- or seven-point scale).

Example:

Please indicate the degree to which you agree or disagree with this statement: *The 1995 Ford 150 Pickup Truck is a substantial improvement over the 1994 model.*

Strongly Agree	Agree	Neither Agree nor Disagree	Disagree	Strongly Disagree
5	4	3	2	1

▶ **Semantic differential.** This method measures attitudes by displaying pairs of opposite terms and asking respondents to check which term better describes their feelings toward the concept or topic. Each pair consists of a positive and negative adjective reflecting the extremes, such as, ''honest-dishonest,'' ''efficient-inefficient,'' ''powerful-weak,'' etc. The adjectives are placed at opposite ends of the line, which is divided into an equal number of segments. Respondents can select the degree to which the adjective describes the topic.

QUESTIONNAIRE DESIGN AND SURVEY ADMINISTRATION (continued)

Example:

Place an X in the space between the two terms that best describes how you see the rods reflecting the *XYZ Corporation District Office.* Mark only one space between each pair of words.

XYZ CORPORATION DISTRICT OFFICE

[the topic or entity being evaluated]

Pleasant	:___:___:___:___:___:___:___:	Unpleasant
Efficient	:___:___:___:___:___:___:___:	Inefficient
Not helpful	:___:___:___:___:___:___:___:	Helpful
Professional	:___:___:___:___:___:___:___:	Unprofessional
Good communicators	:___:___:___:___:___:___:___:	Poor communicators
Insensitive	:___:___:___:___:___:___:___:	Sensitive
Friendly	:___:___:___:___:___:___:___:	Unfriendly
Slow	:___:___:___:___:___:___:___:	Fast
Rigid	:___:___:___:___:___:___:___:	Flexible
Values oriented	:___:___:___:___:___:___:___:	Rules oriented

It is important to reverse some of the items so that people don't develop a "response set"—marking the same column out of habit. In this example, you see some positive terms on the left column and some on the right column.

The advantage of using either the Likert or the semantic differential scales is that you can calculate a number that reflects attitudes and opinions. The values for each scale can then be added together to get a measure of a person's attitudes toward the subject. Also, the researcher can calculate the mean attitude score for one group and compare it with the group or remeasure the same people at a later time to see if shifts in attitudes have occurred.

Exercise: Match Game

Match the following survey item with its correct name:

  a. **Closed-end question**
  b. **Open-end question**
  c. **Checklist**
  d. **Multiple-choice question**
  e. **Ranking scale**
  f. **Likert scale**
  g. **Semantic differential**

_____ **1.** How long have you been shopping here at Happy Jack's?

_____ **2.** When you consider where to shop, what one factor most influences your decision?

  __ location   __ store cleanliness   __ prices

  __ friendliness   __ selection   __ meat quality

_____ *3.* What is the most important three considerations in selecting a super-market. Place a 1 by the most important, a 2 by the second most important and a 3 by the third most important.

  __ location   __ store cleanliness   __ prices

  __ friendliness   __ selection   __ meat quality

_____ **4.** Check each of the following that describe why you shop with Happy Jack's:

  __ location   __ store cleanliness   __ prices

  __ friendliness   __ selection   __ meat quality

_____ **5.** Happy ____ ____ ____ ____ ____ ____ ____ Sad

_____ **6.** Happy Jack's is the best supermarket in Chicago:

  Strongly Agree   1   2   3   4   5   6   7   Strongly Disagree

_____ **7.** Why do you shop at Happy Jack's?

Answers:
1. a   2. d   3. e   4. c   5. g   6. f   7. b.

QUESTIONNAIRE DESIGN AND SURVEY ADMINISTRATION (continued)

STEP 2: Draft and Develop the Questions

The two most important considerations in developing questions are validity and reliability. Validity is the degree to which the item measures what the researcher wants to measure. Reliability is the degree to which the item is likely to get the same results consistently.

One method of improving validity is to be assured that the question will not produce a biased response. Emotionally packed words and questions that lead the respondent toward an obviously preferred answer should be avoided. Also, validity can be improved by including the same questions phrased differently, each of which is aimed to solicit data about the same topic.

Questions that obtain reasonably consistent results when administered to similar samples (or the same sample at different times) are said to be reliable.

STEP 3: Test the Questions

Pretest any questionnaire by administering the survey to a small group of people—people similar to those who will be asked to respond to the final version. Responses to the pretest will tell you how well people understand the questions. This feedback will help you refine the questions to eliminate misunderstandings and confusion.

STEP 4: Develop the Complete Questionnaire

Once the questions have been tested, they should be integrated into a clean, straightforward questionnaire that provides clear instructions on how it should be completed.

Numbering each question and all possible responses will help facilitate the coding process, especially if a computer is used for analysis. Spreadsheet programs are often sufficient for determining the results, although more sophisticated survey processing software is available.

The simplest way of tallying results from small surveys is to stroke each response on a copy of the questionnaire. This is cheap and efficient so long as the sample is fairly small.

The final version of the questionnaire should be psychologically attractive, leaving ample white space. Don't crowd the information; it'll look imposing to the reader and may reduce the number of responses.

The questionnaire should have as many questions as necessary, but as few as possible. Don't overburden the respondent with trivial items. Leave adequate space for fill-in answers. Nothing is more frustrating than trying to put a five-line response into a space where only several words will fit. (This is especially important when using open-ended questions.)

Responses for multiple-choice questions should be mutually exclusive from the other choices. Each choice is different from the others. Eliminate any ambiguous options.

The questionnaire should be titled and professionally reproduced. An attractively printed survey will be positively received and will yield a higher response rate.

STEP 5: Determine the Sample Size You Need

Here is a simple way to calculate your necessary sample size.

First, determine the approximate size of your population—the large group you are trying to find out something about. Then, to get a respectable accuracy level, you'll need to sample the number of people indicated under the ''Sample'' column. Note: These are the number of completed surveys needed. You'll need to account for people who don't respond by sending enough to get the full sample.

These numbers assume random selection of participants. Also note that you almost never need more than a few hundred responses—even for a population of one million!

QUESTIONNAIRE DESIGN AND SURVEY ADMINISTRATION (continued)

A Sample Size Table for Proportions					
Degree of Accuracy *= ±.05*		*Proportion of* *Sample Size = 0.5*		*Confidence Level* *= 95%*	
Population	*Sample*	*Population*	*Sample*	*Population*	*Sample*
10	9	260	155	3000	340
20	19	300	168	5000	356
40	36	400	196	10000	369
60	52	500	217	20000	376
80	66	700	248	50000	381
100	79	900	269	70000	382
140	102	1000	277	120000	382
180	122	1500	305	160000	383
220	140	2000	322	1,000,000	383

Administering the Survey Questionnaire

The method of administering questionnaires depends on the purpose of the research, the method of sampling, the availability of the sample and the amount of resources available to the researcher. Below are some common administering options.

Administer to a Group

From the researcher's point of view, this is the most efficient means. The instructions and introductory information is given at one time and the completed questionnaires are usually ready for coding within a matter of minutes. This method works well when all the questionnaire participants live locally.

Exercise: Mailed Survey Quick Check

Describe three ways you could improve the probability that a person will answer your mailed survey.

1. _____

   _____

2. _____

   _____

3. _____

   _____

Compare your ideas with the tips presented below.

MAIL THE SURVEY

When the representative sample is geographically dispersed, mail questionnaires will have to be used. In such a circumstance, a good sales letter needs to be developed to motivate the targeted sample to spend the time necessary to complete the questionnaire. In addition, a self-addressed, stamped envelope should be included.

Using the mail almost always results in a low percentage of responses. People feel less obligation to respond to mailed surveys. Some procrastinate and ultimately fail to respond at all. A low response rate can be improved by follow-up letters, but this effort increases costs significantly.

You can improve mail survey response rates by:

1. Including a persuasive letter explaining the benefits of completing the survey.

2. Attach a tangible reward such as a dollar bill, valuable coupon or free booklet. A gift causes people to feel some obligation to complete the survey.

3. Make the mailout look personal. Use handwritten or individually typed names and addresses (rather than labels), a first class postage stamp (not metered mail) and a simple return address on the envelope that causes the reader to be curious about what's in the envelope.

SURVEY APPLICATIONS IN BUSINESS RESEARCH

These survey tools will help the business researcher gather more reliable data for more accurate decision making. After each description and example, note a possible application for your business.

CHECKLISTS

Perhaps the simplest device for collecting survey data is the checklist, or a list of items that the respondent checks off or indicates as appropriate. The checklist can be used as a questionnaire technique or in connection with structured observations. It is easy to develop and simple for the respondent to complete.

Example: Ask customers to check off new flavors of ice cream (or new menu items or new services) they would like you to sell. Give them a reasonably short list to choose from (say five or so).

Your business application: _____

_____

_____

MAIL QUESTIONNAIRES

Mail questionnaires should be used when the information needed can be answered easily and quickly by people who are asked to respond. The population should consist of a group for whom names and addresses can be easily obtained. Examples may be your employees, customers or lists of representative people available from a mail list broker. List brokers are available in all major cities. Look in the yellow pages under "Mailing Lists." These brokers can pinpoint target groups and provide preprinted labels at a reasonable cost. They can also help with your sampling strategy.

Since the mail process can take a while, mail questionnaires can be used only when there is sufficient amount of time available for collecting the data.

If a mail questionnaire is an appropriate research tool for your project, it offers several advantages.

- Respondents can usually be reached at very low cost, especially with a geographically disbursed sample. Costs will include postage, list purchases, printing, envelope stuffing and processing of returned surveys.

- Questionnaires may be sent either to the respondent's home or office.

- Respondents will be in a position to answer the questionnaire at their leisure and therefore the questionnaire may be more complete.

- Interviewer bias is completely eliminated.

- Personal and confidential information can be obtained when an unidentified, unsigned questionnaire is used.

Of course, there are also drawbacks. In addition to the disadvantages suffered by most survey techniques, you may also get skewed data if the only people who answer the survey are those who have strong opinions. (This is a common problem with customer response cards used by many businesses. The only people who bother to fill them out are those who are either very unhappy or unusually pleased with the service.)

Attitude Survey

Questionnaires are generally viewed as providing quantitative (numerical) information. But researchers can also use them to measure qualitative concepts such as opinions and attitudes. This is accomplished primarily through the use of Likert scales and semantic differential questions.

To save time and compare results with established norms, many business managers purchased predesigned opinion surveys from consulting and research firms.

Developing a customized opinion questionnaire can be difficult, requires a great deal of testing and revision and, finally cannot be compared with any existing norm. Consider professionally designed questionnaires if you want data on general topics such as job satisfaction, customer satisfaction or attitudes.

Survey Method Review

1. Determine the specific information needed

2. Determine which survey approach should be used

3. Define the population

4. Obtain a random sample

5. Design survey instrument

6. Pilot test the survey

7. Administer survey to the sample

8. Tabulate and analyze results

9. Make decision

✔ Action Step: My Research Problem

Go back to the business research problem you identified on page 24. Develop a draft questionnaire survey using at least three of the types of surveys described previously.

_____

_____

_____

_____

_____

_____

_____

_____

_____

5

Interview Techniques

"Get your facts first, then you can distort them as much as you please."

—Mark Twain

THE INTERVIEW PROCESS

The interview research technique combines observation and surveys to obtain a level of data that is deeper and richer than either of the two techniques can produce separately. Researchers who use interviews will not only be able to get verbal responses from the subject, but more importantly, will also be in a position to observe the subject's nonverbal behavior. This observed behavior of the interviewee, many times, will be more meaningful than the words alone. To get the best data, your interview must be well designed.

Interview Design

Because interviews are so commonplace, some people underestimate the need for structuring and planning an interview in advance. Too many choose to fly by the seat-of-their-pants, and the data they get may be of little value.

A good interview process calls for the 5 C's:

The 5 C's of Interviewing

1. **Constructing the Interview**
2. **Commencing the Interview**
3. **Conducting the Interview**
4. **Concluding the Interview**
5. **Compiling the data and analyzing the results**

Each of these five steps applies whether you are interviewing one person at a time or a group.

THE INTERVIEW PROCESS (continued)

Constructing the Interview

The first activity before all others is to state in writing your purpose of the interview. Be sure to understand what you want to get from the interview. You will then be ready to construct a list of questions to be asked.

Structured and Unstructured Interviews:

There are two types of interviews— structured and unstructured. A structured interview follows a predetermined line of questioning; an unstructured interview allows participants to freely express thoughts important to them.

A structured interview is rather like an interrogation, while an unstructured interview is more like a conversation. Structured interviews are led by the interviewer; in unstructured situations, the interviewer takes the lead from the interviewee.

There are advantages to both types. The structured interview is more efficient and can get needed data quickly. The unstructured interview can produce new insights into the problem that perhaps weren't even thought of by the interviewer. It can get to respondents' feelings and qualitative data more effectively.

The big difficulty with the unstructured interview is that responses may be hard to record, compile and analyze. Themes usually do emerge, but these are subject to the researcher's interpretation.

The structured interview, on the other hand, keeps the interview on a predetermined track through orderly and planned questions.

Open-ended and Closed-ended Questions:

As with surveys, open-ended questions allow the respondent to answer with more than just a few selected responses. A simple yes-no or other two-choice questions are closed-ended questions. Open-ended questions lead to answers that reflect opinion, attitude and explanations.

Exercise: Phrasing Questions

Try the exercise below to test your understanding of open-ended and closed-ended questions. If the question presented is closed-ended, rewrite it to make it open-ended:

1. Have you had any problems with product quality in the past? (This is closed-ended; it could be answered with yes or no. *[Sample rewrite: What problems with product quality have you had in the past?]* If the answer is none, the respondent may still answer with one word, but is given the opportunity to elaborate.)_____

   _____

2. Do you think our overall service is good or bad? _____

   _____

3. Which approach to boosting our sales is better, A or B? _____

   _____

4. Do you prefer the current compensation program or some other? _____

   _____

5. How many times in the past month have you had to change the filter?

   _____

   _____

Pretesting Is Necessary

Just as with survey questionnaires, an interview guide should be tested to determine if respondents are confused about questions. Two groups of individuals should be asked to respond to the proposed interview guide. The first group should be people just like those who will ultimately be sampled. Use this group to determine if the questions are understood and if the desired information can be obtained.

The second group to pretest is other managers. Solicit the comments of fellow managers or other business people who might be able to respond on the instrument's validity. Ask if these questions seem to be getting at the information needed.

THE INTERVIEW PROCESS (continued)

Use Good Questioning Techniques

Better to ask twice than to lose your way once.

—Danish Proverb

Questions should be clustered topically, asking for information about related items together rather than switching topics abruptly. Also, ask easy questions first and more sensitive questions later in the interview. Once people have answered several questions they will feel some obligation to finish the interview even though they may be uncomfortable with the more personal or sensitive questions. Use language consistent with the local, conversational tone. Avoid biased or emotionally loaded words.

COMMENCING THE INTERVIEW

Begin with a greeting to help establish rapport. Since people often form their basic impressions of one another during the first few minutes of contact, the interviewer should always take the time to create a positive rapport and alleviate the interviewee's nervousness. This can be accomplished by doing the following:

- Introduce yourself

- Use enthusiastic, nonverbal welcoming messages like a smile and a warm handshake

- Make an informal, natural comment about the weather, a positive comment about the person's appearance, brief chit-chat about a noncontroversial current event, etc.

- Use humor to break the ice

After the initial contact, the researcher must motivate the interviewee to cooperate during the interview process. Any rewards that might result from the interview should be mentioned. Rewards may range from something tangible to thanking them for their participation.

1. *Stress the importance of the interviewee's answers,* letting them know that what they say will be carefully considered and will have a critical impact on the problem being studied.

2. *Explain how the interviewee was selected* to avoid any suspicion that they were singled out for some sort of special inspection. This approach is especially important in cases where employees are interviewed about some companywide problem. As with surveys, random selection is an excellent and easily explained process that will put people at ease. Another option for some situations is to interview every member of a particular group (say, a department).

3. *Give the interviewee an orientation to the interview.* Explain the purpose of the interview, the interviewee's role in the interview and how the information will be used.

CONDUCTING THE INTERVIEW

During the interview, the interviewer must be mentally alert to the feedback. If the questions are not clearly understood, ask them in a different way. If the response misses the point or is confusing, probe for clarification in a nonthreatening way. Say, "I'm not clear on what you are saying. Can you help me understand that better?"

Avoid disagreement. If you feel the respondent is saying something out of line or inconsistent with what you know to be true, don't confront. Use careful, probing questions to ask for clarification. Be careful of your tone of voice. Don't put the interviewee in a defensive position. The interviewer should at all times be neutral, assuming the role of a careful but nonjudgmental listener.

The researcher needs to manage the interview time efficiently. Skip trivialities, change the focus when the interviewee develops a monologue, shift the topic when the interviewee starts selling opinions or pressing the interviewer for agreement and, finally, keep the small talk to a minimum but sufficient to maintain rapport.

As the interview progresses, capturing the data becomes very important. This can be accomplished either by efficient note taking, tape recording or both.

THE INTERVIEW PROCESS (continued)

Note-Taking Tips

Here are some tips that can help you improve your note-taking abilities.

► Do not try to record word for word what is said. Jot down key information like names, dates, ages, percentages and relevant figures.

► Don't bury your head in your notes while the respondent talks. Note only major points and follow up key facts and figures.

► Don't be bound to linear, textual notes. Develop a personal shorthand. Use symbols instead of words, circle key thoughts, highlight repeated or emphasized ideas.

► Slow the pace when necessary. Tell the respondent that you want to be sure to record everything clearly. Most people are flattered by your efforts to note what they say carefully.

► Develop your memory by training. Most memory training suggests ways of organizing ideas into patterns that are easy for you to recall.

Using Audio and Video Tape

Audio or video taping of the interview provides an excellent opportunity for detailed data verification. Exact information is recorded rather than some interpretations of it. This information then can be stored indefinitely and referred to as needed.

Using recording equipment has two major disadvantages. First, the presence of recording devices may bias the data by causing the subjects to behave differently than they normally would. This may be overcome by allowing the subjects to get used to the recording device before the important parts of the interview are covered.

The second disadvantage is that the data must still be interpreted by the human listener after it is recorded. This means that the recorded interview requires at least twice as much time as the nonrecorded interview.

In actual practice, most professional interviewers prefer note taking with taped backup, which could be reviewed to clarify specific points.

CONCLUDING THE INTERVIEW

Stop the interview when both people have run out of things to say. When this occurs, the interviewer should summarize what was learned, explain how the information will be used and what actions may be precipitated from the findings. After this, the interviewer should thank the interviewee for the time and effort.

COMPILING THE DATA AND ANALYZING THE RESULTS

The data from closed questions can be easily summarized and analyzed using a form much like a survey. Open-question data is another matter. With open-question information, frequency counts and content analysis should be undertaken.

A frequency count simply notes the number of times the same or closely related comments have occurred. Content analysis should use the following guidelines:

- *Identify common themes.* Be sensitive to subtle nuances and common threads that run through the respondent's answers. If several respondents refer to a product or person with apparent disdain, you may conclude that there is a less than positive feeling toward that product or person.

- *Make certain that the data will support the research conclusions.* A list of supporting evidence for each conclusion should be incorporated into the research. Such evidence lends credibility and strength to any recommendations offered and decisions made.

- *Stay focused on your criteria.* As the research is analyzed, criteria for judging success or effectiveness of the process should be developed.

INTERVIEW FORMATS

Three interview formats are used for business research:

INDIVIDUAL, FACE-TO-FACE

TELEPHONE

GROUP

Advantages and disadvantages of each are described below.

Face-to-Face

The face-to-face or personal interview technique is used most often when complete and comprehensive replies are needed. Since interpersonal communication is made up of words, mannerisms and voice modulation, face-to-face contact provides feedback to the interviewer from all three sources.

Advantages

The advantages of individual, face-to-face interviews include:

- The technique may be the only way to obtain accurate data on complicated or sensitive questions.

- You get fewer refusals and premature interview termination because the respondent is one-on-one with the interviewer.

- The questioning is generally more thorough.

- You can build stronger rapport and better respondent cooperation in this more personalized format.

- The interviewer can get fuller explanations and clarifications by probing (follow-up questions) and observing nonverbal behaviors.

Because of these advantages, face-to-face interviewing by skilled individuals is normally credited as being the most accurate data-gathering research method.

Disadvantages

This technique does have some disadvantages. They include:

- Cost. One-on-one interviewing is the most expensive and time-consuming way to gather information.

- The technique requires skilled interviewers to eliminate interview bias.

- If interviewees have been chosen because of their verbal skills or reputation for candor (as is sometimes the case), the advantage of random sampling can be lost.

- Personal or sensitive information may be withheld because of the recording device or a poor chemistry between interviewer and interviewee.

- Interviewees may not be honest with researchers who are also their bosses.

Telephone Interviewing Technique

We have all been subjected to telephone interviews, especially by polling organizations or market research groups. The telephone allows data gathering without the cost of face-to-face interviewing.

Advantages

The advantages of telephone interviewing include:

- People who are difficult to contact or unwilling to give you the time in person will often be open to a telephone call, especially a long distance call.

- It is much easier to take notes, tape the interview and use a script without the interviewee being distracted.

- The telephone commands attention and privacy and minimizes interruptions that can occur in a face-to-face interview.

- The telephone lets the interviewer come to the point quickly and establish a businesslike climate without the interviewee feeling rushed.

- It is not possible for the respondent to read the interviewer's mannerisms and facial expressions, thus keeping a neutral tone in the questions.

- Telephone interviewing is the least expensive method of gathering data from geographically disbursed people.

- People may be more candid over the phone than in a face-to-face interview.

INTERVIEW FORMATS (continued)

Disadvantages

Some disadvantages of telephone interviews include:

- Telephone interviews tend to be shorter than face-to-face interviews, usually not lasting more than 10–15 minutes. Because of this, research projects that require gathering a large amount of data per contact are not suitable for telephone interviewing.

- The interviewer cannot use props, samples or illustrations as part of the questioning, which rules out complicated questions that would require a demonstration or visual device.

- The telephone interview is limited only to those having phones. For research within a company, for example, this would probably eliminate assembly-line workers or those who work outside.

- The telephone does not allow for personal observations of mannerisms, which are one of the best sources of information during interpersonal communications.

Exercise: Interview Script

Write a draft interview script to gather information about your customers' satisfaction level. Use a variety of open-ended and structured questions. Include an introduction that explains why the survey is being taken.

Introduction: _____

_____

Question 1 _____

_____

Question 2 _____

_____

Question 3 _____

_____

Group Interviews

Three types of group interviews are used successfully to collect good research information: panels, focus groups and nominal groups.

Panels

Panels are groups of 7 to 12 people who share some organizational expertise.

Advantages

- Accuracy of information is high. The combined expertise is better than the ideas of any one member. You achieve synergy.

- Often the same panel is convened on a regular, periodical basis, resulting in continuing growth and refinement of opinions, processes, ideas and products.

Disadvantages

- Panels can be expensive to establish and administer. Taking a group of highly paid experts away from their other work, for example, can be disruptive and costly.

- It is often difficult to organize a representative panel that reflects the concerns and input of all relevant groups.

INTERVIEW FORMATS (continued)

- A continuing panel may develop their own biases that can damage the integrity of the inquiry process. This can happen in panels where group cohesiveness and internal harmony become more important than making tough decisions.

- Panelists may lose enthusiasm for the research. Reports may become careless and incomplete, and attempting to collect too much information from the panel may discourage membership.

Focus Groups

A focus group is normally a randomly selected group of 8 to 12 customers (they typically do not have expertise in the organization) who are invited to share their observations and ideas with organizational leaders.

Advantages

- The focus group typically brings in outside ideas from the end user of an organization's goods or services—the customer. (The term customer here should be considered to include internal customers within the larger organization.)

- Because the interviewer does not ask questions or record answers in a traditional sense, he or she is free to act as a discussion leader or group moderator whose purpose is to direct and focus the group discussion toward the issues being researched.

- As the focus group discussion begins to evolve, it is hoped that a spontaneous interchange of ideas will result with a wide variety of insightful and useful data.

Disadvantages

- Cost and time. Typically participants are paid to participate or, minimally, given a free dinner or the like.

- Assembling a random sample of participants may be difficult. Some customers don't have the time or inclination to participate.

- Qualitative data received may be difficult to interpret, especially when opposite recommendations are offered by people within the group.

Create a Successful Focus Group Experience

✓ Hold the group on neutral ground—a conference room or an off-site hotel

✓ Notify participants as to the where, when and why of the meeting

✓ Provide a relaxed atmosphere with refreshments; allow participants to interact to break the ice before starting

✓ Seat everyone around the table and explain the purpose, why and how the participants were chosen and how the results of the session will be used

✓ Have all members introduce themselves to loosen up the group and give you feedback on how well each person meets the selected profile

✓ Direct the discussion in a consistent, deductive manner, moving from general ideas or impressions to specifics

✓ Keep the discussion flowing; ask for clarification when necessary and avoid being judgmental and biased

✓ Don't discourage novel or unusual ideas—sometimes these can be very useful

✓ Provide equal opportunity for all members to contribute; passive members should be encouraged to interact

✓ Conclude by indicating that a lot of information has been covered, but solicit comments from anyone who has anything additional to say

✔ *Action Step: Focus Group Plan Development*

Develop a plan for a focus group to deal with your business concern described on page 24:

From what group(s) will participants be selected? _____

_____

How many will be selected from each group? _____

_____

How will they be selected? _____

_____

Who will facilitate the discussion? _____

_____

How will a record of the comments be made? _____

_____

Where and when will the group meet? _____

_____

How will the problem or topic be introduced? _____

Nominal Group

The nominal group technique is a problem-solving or idea-generating research method that gathers individual judgments and combines them to produce the most acceptable decision. It is not a technique for routine meetings, coordination, bargaining or negotiations.

8-Step Nominal Group Process

1. The facilitator states and clarifies the research question to be sure everyone understands.

2. Members silently generate their ideas in writing.

3. A facilitator uses a round-robin approach to recording feedback from group members. Each person gets to present one idea. No comment or discussion is offered at this time.

4. The facilitator records each idea in a few words on a flip chart or marker board.

5. Participants may discuss each recorded idea for clarification and evaluation.

6. Group members vote on priority ideas. The group decision is mathematically derived through rank ordering. (See example ranking sheet below.)

7. The top-ranked ideas are discussed for no longer than 10 minutes solely to clarify statements.

8. After the discussion of the initial rankings, each individual makes final rankings of the listed ideas by choosing the five most important items from the flip chart and listing them in rank order on sheets of paper. All sheets are then collected and rankings posted.

Sample Nominal Group Ranking Sheet

Suppose that your nominal group has six participants. They have been asked to rank four ideas for improving customer service. The numbers following each idea are the rankings. To get an overall ranking, simply add the numbers. The lowest score is the top-ranked idea.

1. Change employee pay to reward service   1 2 1 4 2 1 = 11

2. Provide additional in-house training   2 1 2 2 3 2 = 12

3. Send employees to Trainco Seminars   3 3 3 1 1 4 = 15

4. Develop new ad slogans   4 4 4 3 4 3 = 22

The first option is ranked overall as the best, although number two is a close second. Perhaps the group will want to consider a combination of one and two.

INTERVIEW FORMATS (continued)

Advantages

- Provides a way to sharpen a focus on the crucial elements of an issue or challenge when there is a lack of agreement or incomplete knowledge concerning the nature of a research problem.

- Maintains the advantages of both individual thinking and the group process. Members alternate between silently thinking of ideas, listing them on a flip chart and then voting on the listed ideas. An objective decision of the group is secured by ranking or rating the ideas.

- Moves the group toward a decision and reduces the probability of it getting bogged down.

Disadvantages

- Process is time consuming.

- It sometimes forces a decision prematurely. By ranking among the alternatives presented, it prohibits generation of new ideas.

- The nominal group requires extensive preparation by the facilitator to identify the information desired from the group and to obtain the necessary supplies.

- The inflexibility of the process forces a focus on a specific topic, which makes adjustments or alterations during the middle of the meeting difficult.

The best part of the nominal group technique is that it gives attention to each idea and increases the opportunity for participation. Each member of the nominal group has a full opportunity (an obligation, really) to participate—even more so than in focus or panel groups. In other group interviewing techniques, discussions may succumb to the dominance of a few individuals who hold special status or have more persuasive personalities. The nominal group's voting procedure can greatly reduce such dominance by aggregating individual judgments into group decisions.

6

Experiments
and Tests

"All life is an experiment. The more experiments you make the better."

—Ralph Waldo Emerson

EFFECTIVE TESTS AND EXPERIMENTS

The foremost rule of effective marketing applies for many other business functions. Simply stated, it says, ''The three most important marketing activities are testing, testing and testing.'' Never assume that what has always worked will continue to work. Business success is a constant process of evaluation and improvement. Testing is the research technique that can best help you keep a finger on the pulse of all aspects of organizational success.

Experiments can be the most reliable and accurate of all the research procedures. They are not used to solicit opinions or ideas from people; rather, they are used to determine results of organizational decisions. They don't measure what is said, believed, or felt but what happens when a change is introduced into the equation.

Effective experiments yield hard facts, produce results, and function in reality. Because of the type of information generated by experiments and tests, they are the most powerful business research method to project future results.

ADVANTAGES

- Experiments and tests are the most reliable and accurate of all research methods

- The use of control groups greatly reduces errors from outside, unforeseen factors

- Several factors or variables may be tested at the same time

- Running carefully designed experiments can be fun and gives the researcher a great deal of credibility

DISADVANTAGES

- Cost

- Expertise in research design needed to isolate variables and create comparable situations

THE GAME IS TO CONTROL THE VARIABLES

The secret in putting together a successful experiment is to keep all the variables—or anything that could possibly be a variable—constant except the one under investigation. For example, let's say you are interested in determining the cost effectiveness of a new direct mail advertising piece. This new mailout includes a different "call-to-action" incentive for the customer. Let's say that it offers customers who respond within 10 days a "buy one, get one free" deal.

The important thing that needs to be done here is to control all extraneous variables and to make sure that the only difference measured is the buy one, get one free incentive.

This sounds easy, but can be a difficult thing to do. To test this offer, we would need to keep the following variables constant:

► Sales message

► Document layout

► Printing and paper quality

► Mailing schedule (pieces would have to be mailed on the same days of the week or month)

► Postage amount

► Mailing lists (each approach would be equal and any one prospect in the target market would have an equal chance of receiving either offer)

Exercise: Identify Other Variables

List any other factors that might have a contaminating effect on the experiment (there are others!):

1. _____

2. _____

3. _____

4. _____

5. _____

ANSWERS: Other possible contaminants could be:

- hand addressed vs. mailing label, postage stamp vs. metered or bulk rate mail, printing quality, typefaces, colors used, return address, bulletin offer on envelope, failure to randomize sample

IN SEARCH OF VALIDITY AND RELIABILITY

You'll want your experiment to have both validity and reliability. An experiment is valid when the results actually measure what is supposed to be measured—in our example, the different effects of the incentive offer. By controlling variables, you can be reasonably sure that a result from a test is due to the test variable. Such a result would be valid.

Reliability is the probability that you would get the same results if the experiment were repeated in the same way. Our experiment would have reliability if the results can be duplicated consistently; that is, every time we use the buy one, get one free offer, the results will be greater or lesser than from other mailouts. Fortunately, both validity and reliability can be increased through proper experiment design.

It's All In the Design

Taking our example of testing a new incentive offer, let's look at some design approaches we can use to help build reliability and validity into our experiment on the new mailer. The first and most common test method used is what might be called the "Let's Give It a Try" approach LGIT.

Using LGIT, we would send out our whole mailing with the new offer and then compare the results with the mailing we used last time.

Can you see any problems with this approach? _____

_____

What are they? _____

_____

LGIT may be appropriate when only a minor change or adjustment is involved. It is consistent with the "ready, fire, aim" management style that encourages constant innovation. It can be fun to try out something new in a casual way if the downside risk is minimal. Rearranging a display in a store or putting impulse buy items near a cash register are examples of LGIT tests.

When the risk of poor results is potentially costly (say our mailing example costs tens of thousands of dollars and will be repeated regularly), a more carefully designed experiment is called for.

The LGIT approach would not be a true experiment for our mailout example for many possible reasons, including:

- Your new mailing went out on a different day of the week than the older one.

- Your new mailing list has more qualified names and is more productive.

- A competitor sent out a mailing with a better incentive offer just two days before yours.

The real problem with the LGIT design is that the experimental variable was introduced without a control (comparison) group or without any specific prior knowledge about the individuals who received the mailer. This does not allow us to evaluate the effectiveness of the mailing and make a valid comparison between two offers.

The "Before and After" (B/A) experiment design would be an improvement. In this case we would send two mailings—one with the incentive and one without—to the same individuals at different times. The results could then be compared. This is an improvement over LGIT, but not by much. The timing reduces accuracy, because all kinds of errors can creep into the experiment. Change occurs over time and introduces factors that will contaminate the results. One obvious possibility is a situation in which the customer accepts the nonincentive offer and then gets a better offer for the same product a few months later. Hard feelings could result.

The Solution to Validity and Reliability

The solution to our research design question is to introduce the concepts of randomization and control groups. These techniques will help us to minimize any errors introduced into the experiment. Randomization as described earlier is the act of selecting a subset from the target population in such a way that any one individual case in the population has an equal chance of being selected.

A control group is a randomly selected sample that is used as the benchmark. This group's results will act as the basis for comparison between the two offers. A control group is selected at the same time, in the same manner and from the population as is the experimental group.

IN SEARCH OF VALIDITY AND RELIABILITY (continued)

The example shows the design for a test of two approaches and two prices. This marketing company wants to know which of two mailing pieces works best and which of two prices attracts the most customers. They try a two-page mailout and a four-page mailout. They also try pricing at $149 and $179. The tallies show the number of customers for each combination.

Marketing Comparison

	2-page ad	4-page ad
$179	////	⫽⫽⫽ ⫽⫽⫽ ///
$149	⫽⫽⫽ ⫽⫽⫽ ///	⫽⫽⫽ ⫽⫽⫽ ⫽⫽⫽ /

The use of such a box quickly points to the most successful of the options available. In this case it is clear that the two-page ad at $179 is inferior to the other options. The other options should be calculated to determine the revenue generated as shown in the figure below. We multiplied the number of responses by the price to get the sales dollars. Assume the two-page ad costs $.15 ea, the four-page ad costs $.21 and 1,000 pieces were mailed for each of the four approaches. Here are the profit margins:

	Sales Dollars Received	Cost of Ads	Net Revenue
A	4 responses @ $179 = $716	$150	$566
B	13 responses @ $179 = $2327	$210	$2117
C	13 responses @ $149 = $1937	$150	$1787
D	16 responses @ $149 = $2384	$210	$2174

Assuming that the sample is representative of the population—that the same results will consistently appear from similar mailings—which is the best option?

The best option is _____.

A FINAL THOUGHT

Obviously a small book like this one cannot make you an expert researcher. Our intention is more modest: We hope that after reading this book you will improve your abilities to think like a researcher.

Business success is a process of consistently looking for better options, for better ways to perform business functions. A critical, evaluative eye is a great management asset. Look carefully and systematically at all that you are doing. Refer often to this book as your informal guide to business research.

APPENDIX

A Sample Research Instrument

"Originality is the art of concealing your source."

—Thomas Edison

ORGANIZATIONAL COMMUNICATION QUESTIONNAIRE SURVEY

by The International Communication Association

This survey instrument applies many of the ideas in this book. The following organizational audit was created by the International Communication Association. This instrument is available for your use without charge and provides a great deal of useful information about organizational effectiveness. It is included here as an example of an in-depth survey instrument.

Instructions

Please mark all your responses on the enclosed answer sheet. Please use the pencil supplied, as ink or hard lead pencils will not be recorded. Also, please carefully erase any stray pencil marks. Please answer all questions since each is important for possibly improving the operation of your organization. If there are any questions which do not apply to you, leave them blank. If there are questions which you do not understand, please ask us about them. We appreciate your patience for this important survey.

PLEASE MARK ONLY ONE RESPONSE TO EACH QUESTION

Receiving Information from Others

Instructions for Questions 1 through 26

You can receive information about various topics in your organization. For each topic listed on the following pages, mark your response on the answer sheet that best indicates: (1) the amount of information you *are* receiving on that topic and (2) the amount of information you *need* to receive on that topic, that is, the amount you *have to have* in order to do your job.

QUESTIONNAIRE SURVEY (continued)

Topic Area	This is the amount of information I receive now					This is the amount of information I need to receive				
	Very Little	Little	Some	Great	Very Great	Very Little	Little	Some	Great	Very Great
How well I am doing in my job.	**1.** 1	2	3	4	5	**2.** 1	2	3	4	5
My job duties.	**3.** 1	2	3	4	5	**4.** 1	2	3	4	5
Organizational policies.	**5.** 1	2	3	4	5	**6.** 1	2	3	4	5
Pay and benefits	**7.** 1	2	3	4	5	**8.** 1	2	3	4	5
How technological changes affect my job	**9.** 1	2	3	4	5	**10.** 1	2	3	4	5
Mistakes and failures of my organization.	**11.** 1	2	3	4	5	**12.** 1	2	3	4	5
How I am being judged.	**13.** 1	2	3	4	5	**14.** 1	2	3	4	5
How my job-related problems are being handled.	**15.** 1	2	3	4	5	**16.** 1	2	3	4	5
How organization decisions are made that affect my job.	**17.** 1	2	3	4	5	**18.** 1	2	3	4	5
Promotion and advancement opportunities in my organization.	**19.** 1	2	3	4	5	**20.** 1	2	3	4	5
Important new product, service or program developments in my organization.	**21.** 1	2	3	4	5	**22.** 1	2	3	4	5
How my job relates to the total operation of my organization.	**23.** 1	2	3	4	5	**24.** 1	2	3	4	5
Specific problems faced by management.	**25.** 1	2	3	4	5	**26.** 1	2	3	4	5

Sending Information to Others

Instructions for Questions 27 through 40

In addition to receiving information, there are many topics on which you can send information to others. For each topic listed on the following pages, mark your response on the answer sheet that best indicates: (1) the amount of information you *are* sending on that topic and (2) the amount of information you *need* to send on that topic in order to do your job.

Topic Area		This is the amount of information I send now						This is the amount of information I need to send now				
		Very Little	Little	Some	Great	Very Great		Very Little	Little	Some	Great	Very Great
Reporting what I am doing in my job	27.	1	2	3	4	5	28.	1	2	3	4	5
Reporting what I think my job requires me to do	29.	1	2	3	4	5	30.	1	2	3	4	5
Reporting job-related problems	31.	1	2	3	4	5	32.	1	2	3	4	5
Complaining about my job and/or working conditions	33.	1	2	3	4	5	34.	1	2	3	4	5
Requesting information necessary to do my job	35.	1	2	3	4	5	36.	1	2	3	4	5
Evaluating the performance of my immediate supervisor	37.	1	2	3	4	5	38.	1	2	3	4	5
Asking for clearer work instructions	39.	1	2	3	4	5	40.	1	2	3	4	5

QUESTIONNAIRE SURVEY (continued)

Follow-up on Information Sent

Instructions for Questions 41 through 50

Indicate the amount of *action* or *follow-up* that *is* and *needs* to be taken on information you send to the following:

	This is the amount of follow-up now					This is the amount of follow-up needed				
Topic Area	Very Little	Little	Some	Great	Very Great	Very Little	Little	Some	Great	Very Great
Subordinates	41. 1	2	3	4	5	42. 1	2	3	4	5
Co-workers	43. 1	2	3	4	5	44. 1	2	3	4	5
Immediate supervisor	45. 1	2	3	4	5	46. 1	2	3	4	5
Middle Management	47. 1	2	3	4	5	48. 1	2	3	4	5
Top Management	49. 1	2	3	4	5	50. 1	2	3	4	5

Sources of Information

Instructions for Questions 51 through 68

You *not only* receive various kinds of information, but can receive such information from *various sources* within the organization. For each source listed below, mark your response on the answer sheet that best indicates: (1) the amount of information you *are* receiving from that source and (2) the amount of information you *need* to receive from that source in order to do your job.

Sources of Information	*This is the amount of information I receive now*						*This is the amount of information I need to receive*				
		Very Little	Little	Some	Great	Very Great		Very Little	Little	Some	Great	Very Great
Subordinates (if applicable)	51.	1	2	3	4	5	52.	1	2	3	4	5
Co-workers in my own unit or department	53.	1	2	3	4	5	54.	1	2	3	4	5
Individuals in *other* units, departments in my organization	55.	1	2	3	4	5	56.	1	2	3	4	5
Immediate supervisor	57.	1	2	3	4	5	58.	1	2	3	4	5
Department meetings	59.	1	2	3	4	5	60.	1	2	3	4	5
Middle Management	61.	1	2	3	4	5	62.	1	2	3	4	5
Formal management presentations	63.	1	2	3	4	5	64.	1	2	3	4	5
Top management	65.	1	2	3	4	5	66.	1	2	3	4	5
The "grapevine"	67.	1	2	3	4	5	68.	1	2	3	4	5

QUESTIONNAIRE SURVEY (continued)

Timeliness of Information Received from Key Sources

Instructions for Questions 69 to 74

Indicate the extent to which information from the following sources is usually *timely* (you get information when you need it—not too early, not too late).

		Very Little	Little	Some	Great	Very Great
Subordinates (if applicable)	69.	1	2	3	4	5
Co-workers	70.	1	2	3	4	5
Immediate supervisor	71.	1	2	3	4	5
Middle Management	72.	1	2	3	4	5
Top Management	73.	1	2	3	4	5
"Grapevine"	74.	1	2	3	4	5

Organizational Communication Relationships

Instructions for Questions 75 through 93

A variety of communicative relationships exist in organizations like your own. Employees exchange messages regularly with supervisors, subordinates, co-workers, etc. Considering your relationships with others in your organization, please mark your response on the answer sheet which best describes the relationship in question.

Relationship:		Very Little	Little	Some	Great	Very Great
I trust my co-workers	75.	1	2	3	4	5
My co-workers get along with each other	76.	1	2	3	4	5
My relationship with my co-workers is satisfying	77.	1	2	3	4	5
I trust my immediate supervisor	78.	1	2	3	4	5
My immediate supervisor is honest with me	79.	1	2	3	4	5
My immediate supervisor listens to me	80.	1	2	3	4	5
I am free to disagree with my immediate supervisor	81.	1	2	3	4	5
I can tell my immediate supervisor when things are going wrong	82.	1	2	3	4	5
My immediate supervisor praises me for a good job	83.	1	2	3	4	5
My immediate supervisor is friendly with his/her subordinates	84.	1	2	3	4	5
My immediate supervisor understands my job needs	85.	1	2	3	4	5
My relationship with my immediate supervisor is satisfying	86.	1	2	3	4	5
I trust top management	87.	1	2	3	4	5
Top management is sincere in their efforts to communicate with employees	88.	1	2	3	4	5
My relationship with top management is satisfying	89.	1	2	3	4	5
My organization encourages differences of opinion	90.	1	2	3	4	5
I have a say in decisions that affect my job	91.	1	2	3	4	5
I influence operations in my unit or department	92.	1	2	3	4	5
I have a part in accomplishing my organization's goals	93.	1	2	3	4	5

QUESTIONNAIRE SURVEY (continued)

Organizational Outcomes

Instructions for Questions 94 through 106

One of the most important "outcomes" of working in an organization is the *satisfaction* one receives or fails to receive through working there. Such "satisfaction" can relate to the job, one's co-workers, supervisor, or the organization as a whole. Please mark your response on the answer sheet which best indicates the extent to which you are satisfied with:

Outcome:		Very Little	Little	Some	Great	Very Great
My job	94.	1	2	3	4	5
My pay	95.	1	2	3	4	5
My progress in my organization up to this point in time	96.	1	2	3	4	5
My chances for getting ahead in my organization	97.	1	2	3	4	5
My opportunity to "make a difference"—to contribute to the overall success of my organization	98.	1	2	3	4	5
My organization's system for recognizing and rewarding outstanding performance	99.	1	2	3	4	5
My organization's concern for its members' welfare	100.	1	2	3	4	5
My organization's overall communicative efforts	101.	1	2	3	4	5
Working in my organization	102.	1	2	3	4	5
My organization, as compared to other such organizations	103.	1	2	3	4	5
My organization's overall efficiency of operation	104.	1	2	3	4	5
The overall quality of my organization's product or service	105.	1	2	3	4	5
My organization's achievement of its goals and objectives	106.	1	2	3	4	5

Channels of Communication

Instructions for Questions 107 through 122

The following questions list a variety of channels through which information is transmitted to employees. Please mark your response on the answer sheet which best indicates: (1) the amount of information you *are* receiving through that channel and (2) the amount of information you *need* to receive through that channel.

Channel:	*This is the amount of information I receive now*						*This is the amount of information I need to receive*				
		Very Little	Little	Some	Great	Very Great		Very Little	Little	Some	Great	Very Great
Face-to-face contact between two people	107.	1	2	3	4	5	108.	1	2	3	4	5
Face-to-face contact among more than two people	109.	1	2	3	4	5	110.	1	2	3	4	5
Telephone	111.	1	2	3	4	5	112.	1	2	3	4	5
Written (memos, letters)	113.	1	2	3	4	5	114.	1	2	3	4	5
Bulletin Boards	115.	1	2	3	4	5	116.	1	2	3	4	5
Internal Publications (newsletter, magazine)	117.	1	2	3	4	5	118.	1	2	3	4	5
Internal Audio-Visual Media Videotape, Films, Slides)	119.	1	2	3	4	5	120.	1	2	3	4	5
External Media (TV, Radio, Newspapers)	121.	1	2	3	4	5	122.	1	2	3	4	5

COMMUNICATION AUDIT
COMMUNICATIVE EXPERIENCE FORM

While you were filling out the previous section, the questions may have brought to mind a recent work-related experience of yours in which *communication* was particularly ineffective or effective. Please answer the questions below and give us a clearly printed summary of that experience.

A. To whom does this experience primarily relate? (circle *one*)

1. Subordinate   **2.** Co-worker   **3.** Immediate supervisor

4. Middle management   **5.** Top management

B. Please rate the quality of communication described in the experience below (circle *one*):

1. Effective   **2.** Ineffective

C. To what item in the *previous section* does this experience *primarily* relate?

_____ (Put in the item number)

Describe the communicative experience, the circumstances leading up to it, what the person did that made him/her an effective communicator, and the results (outcome) of what the person did. PLEASE *PRINT*. THANK YOU.

_____

_____

_____

_____

_____

_____

_____

_____

_____

_____

_____

_____

BACKGROUND INFORMATION

This section is for statistical purposes only and will be used to study how different groups of people view your organization. We do not want your name, but would appreciate the following information.

123. How do you receive most of your income from this organization?

 1. Salaried
 2 Hourly
 3. Piece work
 4. Commission
 5. Other

124. What is your sex?

 1. Male
 2. Female

125. Do you work:

 1. Full-time
 2. Part-time
 3. Temporary Full-time
 4. Temporary Part-time

126. How long have you worked in this organization?

 1. Less than 1 year
 2. 1 to 5 years
 3. 6 to 10 years
 4. 11 to 15 years
 5. More than 15 years

127. How long have you held your present position?

 1. Less than 1 year
 2. 1 to 5 years
 3. 6 to 10 years
 4. 11 to 15 years
 5. More than 15 years

128. What is your position in this organization?

 1. I don't supervise anybody
 2. First-line supervisor
 3. Middle management
 4. Top management
 5. Other (Please specify: _____)

BACKGROUND INFORMATION (continued)

130. What is your age?

    1. Under 20 years of age
    2. 21 to 30 years of age
    3. 31 to 40 years of age
    4. 41 to 50 years of age
    5. Over 50 years of age

131. How much training to improve your communicative skills have you had?

    1. No training at all
    2. Little training (attended one seminar, workshop, training activity or course)
    3. Some training (attended a few seminars, workshops, training activities, or courses)
    4. Extensive training (attended a great number of seminars, workshops, training activities, or courses)

132. How much money did you receive from this organization last year?

    1. Less than 12,500
    2. 12,500 to 19,999
    3. 20,000 to 29,999
    4. 30,000 to 39,999
    5. 40,000 to 49,999
    6. over 50,000

133. During the past ten years, in how many other organizations have you been employed?

    1. No other organizations
    2. One other organization
    3. Two other organizations
    4. Three other organizations
    5. More than three others

134. Are you presently looking for a job in a different organization?

    _____ Yes

    _____ No

OVER 150 BOOKS AND 35 VIDEOS AVAILABLE IN THE 50-MINUTE SERIES

We hope you enjoyed this book. If so, we have good news for you. This title is part of the best-selling *50-MINUTE*™ *Series* of books. All *Series* books are similar in size and identical in price. Many are supported with training videos.

To order *50-MINUTE* Books and Videos or request a free catalog, contact your local distributor or Crisp Publications, Inc., 1200 Hamilton Court, Menlo Park, CA 94025. Our toll-free number is (800) 442-7477.

50-Minute Series Books and Videos Subject Areas . . .

Management
Training
Human Resources
Customer Service and Sales Training
Communications
Small Business and Financial Planning
Creativity
Personal Development
Wellness
Adult Literacy and Learning
Career, Retirement and Life Planning

Other titles available from Crisp Publications in these categories

Crisp Computer Series
The Crisp Small Business & Entrepreneurship Series
Quick Read Series
Management
Personal Development
Retirement Planning